# ENGLISH TOWN

## FOR EVERYONE

BOOK

**3**

# Contents

## Hello Song

Hello, everyone.
Hello, teacher!
Hello, friends!

Let's have fun together.
We'll have a good time.

Are you ready to start?
We're ready!

Here we go!

## Goodbye Song

Did you have fun?

It's time to say goodbye.
See you next time!
See you next time!

Did you enjoy the class?
Yes! We had a fun time!
Yes! We had a fun time!

See you later! See you later!
Goodbye. Goodbye.

Bye! Bye!

# Lesson 1

# Choosing a Restaurant

Let's Talk

## A. Look, listen, and repeat.

Let's eat out.

Okay.

Which restaurant do you want to go to?

I want to go to an Italian restaurant.

Let's eat out.

Sure, let's go.

Which restaurant do you want to go to?

I want to go to an Italian restaurant.

ACT IT OUT

Okay.

## B. Listen and practice.

I want to go to an Italian restaurant.

① Italian     ② Chinese     ③ Indian     ④ Japanese

## C. Listen, point, and say.

A: Which restaurant do you want to go to?
B: I want to go to an Italian restaurant.

## A. Listen and chant.

Mom, Mom!

Let's eat out! Let's eat out!

   Okay, okay!

   Which restaurant do you want to go to?

   Want to go to?

Italian, Italian, Italian!

I want to go to an Italian restaurant!

## B. Read and write the numbers.

  I want to go to an Indian restaurant.

  I want to go to an Italian restaurant.

  I want to go to a Japanese restaurant.

  I want to go to a Chinese restaurant.

## C. Match, ask, and answer.

> A: Which restaurant do you want to go to?
> B: I want to go to an Italian restaurant.

① ② ③

Italian   Japanese   Indian   Chinese   Korean   Mexican

④ ⑤ ⑥

## D. Work with your friends.

- Which restaurant do you want to go to? Ask your friends and write their names.

Chinese   Name: _____

Korean   Name: _____

Indian   Name: _____

Mexican   Name: _____

## Lesson 2 At the Restaurant

Let's Talk

### A. Look, listen, and repeat.

Are you ready to order?

Yes, I am.

I would like a salad.

Okay.

Are you ready to order?

Yes, I am.

Okay.

I would like some spaghetti and meatballs.

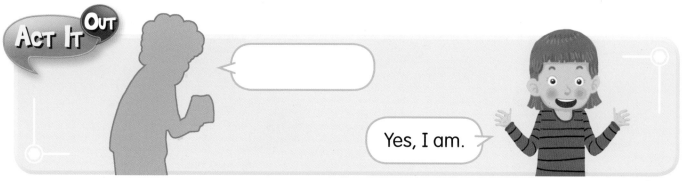

**ACT IT OUT**

Yes, I am.

10

**B.** Listen and practice.

I would like some salad.

**①**

**②**

**③**

**④**

salad

spaghetti and
meatballs

potato pizza

garlic bread

A: I would like some spaghetti and meatballs.
B: Okay.

**C.** Listen, point, and say.

**Let's Learn**

## A. Listen and chant.

Are you ready to order?

Yes! Yes! Yes, I am.

I would like a salad! Salad! Salad!

Okay. Good.

Are you ready to order?

Yes! Yes! Yes, I am.

I would like some garlic bread!

Garlic bread! Garlic bread!

Okay. Good.

## B. Listen and match.

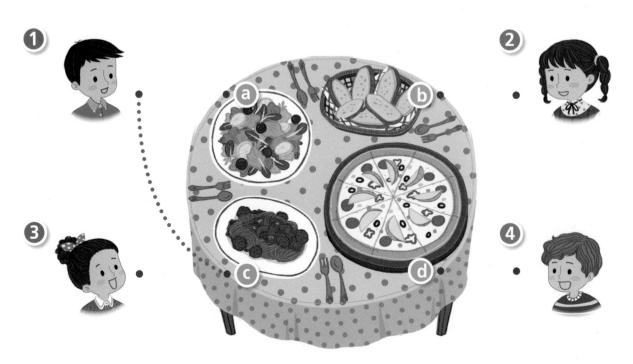

1
2
3
4

a
b
c
d

## C. Go down the ladder.
## Then, ask and answer.

A: I would like some salad.
B: Okay.

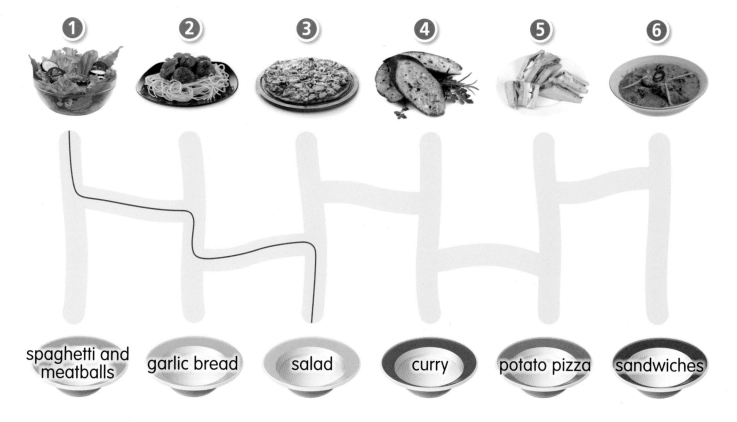

① ② ③ ④ ⑤ ⑥

spaghetti and meatballs  garlic bread  salad  curry  potato pizza  sandwiches

## D. Work with your friends.

- Draw the food you would like and tell the class.

I would like some potato pizza.

# Kero Is at an Italian Restaurant

**A.** Listen and repeat.

**B.** Listen and number the pictures.

Kero

Kiki

## C. Read and circle.

Which restaurant do they want to go to?

- Kero 👓 wants to go to ( an Italian, a Chinese ) restaurant.
- Kiki 🐱 wants to go to ( an Italian, a Chinese ) restaurant.

## D. Choose the restaurant you want to go to and do a role-play.

## A. Listen and sing.

### Let's Eat Out

Let's eat out today.
Okay! Okay!
Which restaurant do you want to go to?
　I want to go to an Italian restaurant.
Which restaurant do you want to go to?
　I want to go to an Indian restaurant.

　Are you ready to order?
　　Yes, I would like a salad.
　Are you ready to order?
　　Yes, I would like some curry.

## B. Play bingo.

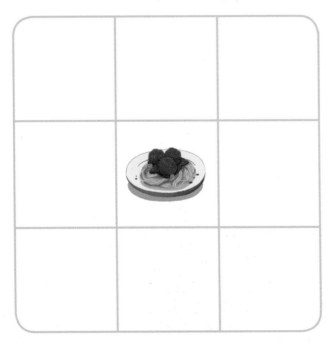

I would like some spaghetti and meatballs.

e-learning

# The World's Popular Foods

Croissant from France

Each country has its own food.

Many Korean people eat out these days.

What's your favorite food?

Which restaurant do you want to go to?

Look at some popular foods around the world.

They look really delicious!

Sushi from Japan

Napoli Pizza from Italy

Curry from India

Tacos from Mexico

Doughnuts from the USA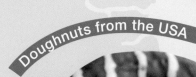

### Check It Out!

1. Where does sushi come from?

2. Which restaurant do you want to go to for lunch?

## Table Manners

**Let's Talk**

### A. Look, listen, and repeat.

Don't speak with your mouth full.

Okay.

Pass me the salt, please.

Sure.

Okay.

Cover your mouth when you cough.

Pass me a napkin, please.

Sure.

**ACT IT OUT**

Okay.

18

## B. Listen and practice.

Pass me the salt, please.

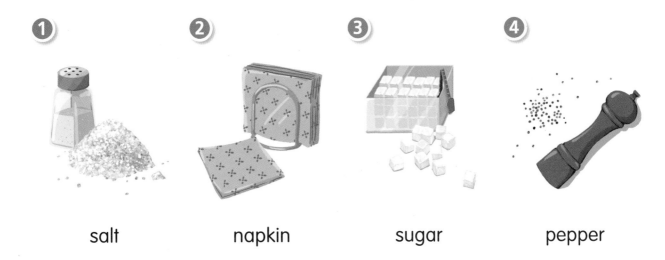

① salt

② napkin

③ sugar

④ pepper

## C. Listen, point, and say.

A: Pass me the salt, please.
B: Sure.

Let's Learn

## A. Listen and chant.

Pass me the salt, please.

Salt, salt, salt.

Don't speak with your mouth full.

Don't, don't, don't.

Okay, okay. I'm so sorry.

Pass me a napkin, please.

Napkin, napkin, napkin.

Cover your mouth when you cough.

Cover, cover, cover.

Okay, okay. I'm so sorry.

## B. Listen and number.

a  ◯

b  ◯

c  ◯

d  ◯

## C. Match, ask, and answer.

A: Pass me the salt, please.
B: Sure.

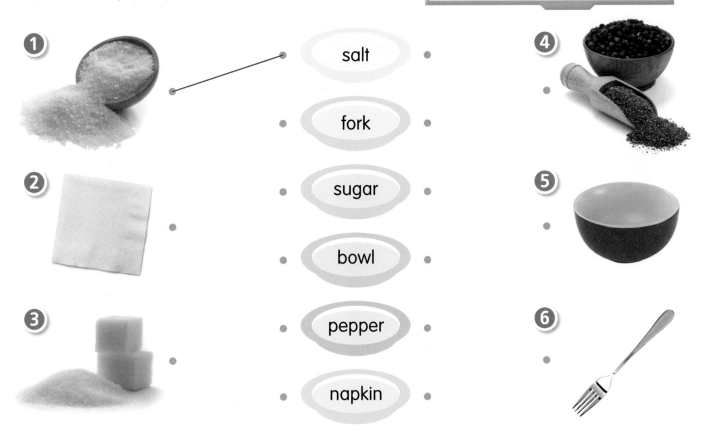

① salt

② fork

③ sugar

bowl

pepper

napkin

④

⑤

⑥

## D. Work with your friends.

- Draw the things they need and guess what they say.

Pass me ... .

Lesson 4   **21**

# Asking about Prices

Let's Talk

## A. Look, listen, and repeat.

How was the food?

It was delicious.

How much is it?

It is eighty dollars.

How was the food?

It was good.

How much is it?

BIG SALE 50% OFF

90 dollars

It is ninety dollars.

ACT IT OUT

How was the food?

22

**B. Listen and practice.**

It is eighty dollars.

① $ 80
eighty

② $ 90
ninety

③ $ 100
one hundred

④ $ 120
one hundred twenty

**C. Listen, point, and say.**

A: How much is it?
B: It is eighty dollars.

**Let's Learn**

## A. Listen and chant.

How was the food? It was delicious.
How was the food? It was good.
How much is it?
   Eighty dollars, eighty dollars.
   It's eighty dollars.

How was the food? It was delicious.
How was the food? It was good.
How much is it?
   One hundred dollars, one hundred dollars.
   It's one hundred dollars.

## B. Look, read, and write the prices.

**1** How much is it? eighty

It is _____80_____ dollars.

**2** one hundred

It is _____ dollars.

**3** ninety

It is _____ dollars.

**4** one hundred twenty

It is _____ dollars.

## C. Match, ask, and answer.

A: How much is it?
B: It is eighty dollars.

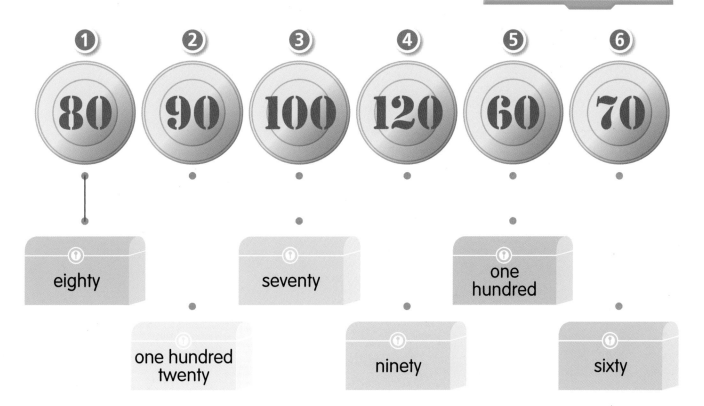

① 80 ② 90 ③ 100 ④ 120 ⑤ 60 ⑥ 70

eighty

seventy

one hundred

one hundred twenty

ninety

sixty

## D. Work with your friends.

- How much would you pay for the following items? Write the prices and compare them with your friends.

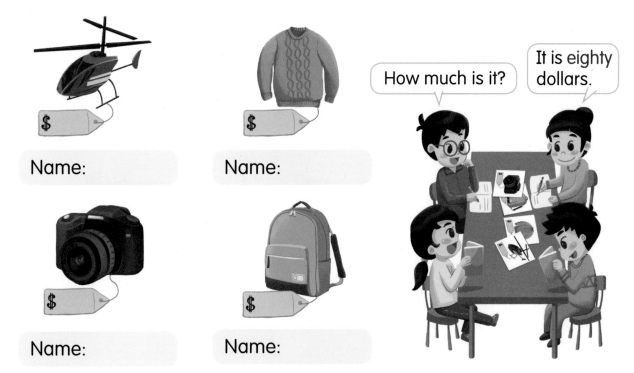

$ Name:

$ Name:

How much is it?

It is eighty dollars.

$ Name:

$ Name:

## Lesson 6

# Don't Speak with Your Mouth Full

**A.** Listen and repeat.

**B.** Listen and number the pictures.

## C. Read and check True or False.

1 Kero speaks with his mouth full. .......................... True ☐  False ☐

2 Dad passes Kero the pepper. .......................... True ☐  False ☐

3 The food was not delicious. .......................... True ☐  False ☐

## D. Choose and do a role-play.

 ☐   ☐   ☐

Lesson 6  **27**

## A. Listen and sing.

Table Manners

Pass me the sugar, please.
Please. ×2
Don't speak with your mouth full.
  Okay. ×2
Cover your mouth when you cough.
Cough. ×2
How was the food?
  It was delicious.
How much is it?
  It is eighty dollars.

## B. Play a board game.

Don't speak ... .

A: How much is it?
B: It is _____ dollars.

Pass me ... .

A: _____ the food?
B: It was delicious.

Pass me ... .

A: How much is it?
B: It is _____ dollars.

Cover ... .

e-learning

# Table Manners

Don't blow your nose.

Take small bites.

There are some common table manners when you have food. Don't speak with your mouth full and cover your mouth when you cough. But there are some differences between countries.

For example, it is very rude to burp during a meal in many countries. But, in some countries, it is okay to do that. What are good table manners in your country? Let's look at the following common good table manners.

Don't complain about the food.

Bring your dishes to the sink when you finish eating.

## Check It Out!

1. Say two common table manners.
2. What other table manners do you know?

# Places to Buy Things

**Let's Talk**

## A. Look, listen, and repeat.

Oh, I have to buy a recorder.

Okay, let's go to buy one.

Where can I buy a recorder?

You can buy one at a music store.

Oh, I have to buy a bat.

Okay, let's go to buy one.

Where can I buy a bat?

You can buy one at a sports shop.

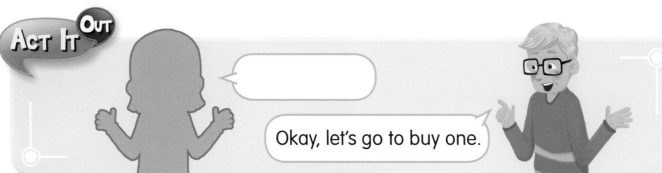

**ACT IT OUT**

Okay, let's go to buy one.

**B. Listen and practice.**

> You can buy one at a music store.

① music store ② sports shop ③ department store ④ stationery store

**C. Listen, point, and say.**

> A: Where can I buy a pencil?
> B: You can buy one at a stationery store.

## A. Listen and chant.

Dad, Dad, I have to buy a recorder.

Okay, okay. Let's go to buy one!

Dad, Dad. Where can I buy a recorder?

Hmm, hmm.

You can buy one at a music store!

Mom, Mom, I have to buy a bat.

Okay, okay. Let's go to buy one!

Mom, Mom. Where can I buy a bat?

Hmm, hmm.

You can buy one at a sports shop!

## B. Read and match.

A: Where can I buy a bag?
B: You can buy one at a department store.

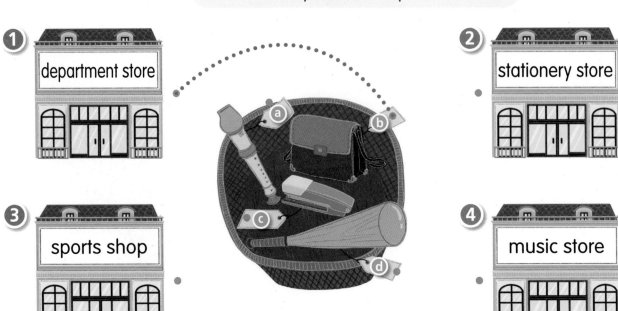

① department store

② stationery store

③ sports shop

④ music store

## C. Ask and answer.

A: Where can I buy a guitar?
B: You can buy one at a music store.

**1**
guitar,
music store

**2**
glove,
sports shop

**3**
scarf,
department store

**4**
notebook,
stationery store

**5**
band-aid,
drugstore

**6**
leash,
pet shop

## D. Work with your friends.

- Write the things you have and tell the class where you can buy them.

| Name | Thing | Place |
|------|-------|-------|
|      |       |       |
|      |       |       |
|      |       |       |
|      |       |       |

Sue, where can I buy an eraser?

You can buy one at a stationery store.

# Places to Find

**Let's Talk**

## A. Look, listen, and repeat.

What can I do for you?

I'm looking for recorders.

Are they in the cabinet?

No, they are in the showcase.

What can I do for you?

I'm looking for bats.

Are they in the box?

No, they are on the shelf.

ACT IT OUT

What can I do for you?

**B. Listen and practice.**

They are in the cabinet.

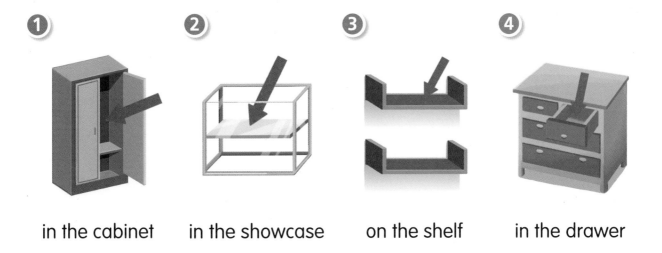

| ① | ② | ③ | ④ |
| --- | --- | --- | --- |
| in the cabinet | in the showcase | on the shelf | in the drawer |

**C. Listen, point, and say.**

A: Are they in the box?
B: No, they are on the shelf.

## Let's Learn

### A. Listen and chant.

What can I do for you?

I'm looking for recorders.

Are they, are they in the cabinet?

No, no. They are in the showcase,

in the showcase.


What can I do for you?

I am looking for bats.

Are they, are they in the box?

No, no. They are on the shelf, on the shelf.

### B. Listen and choose.

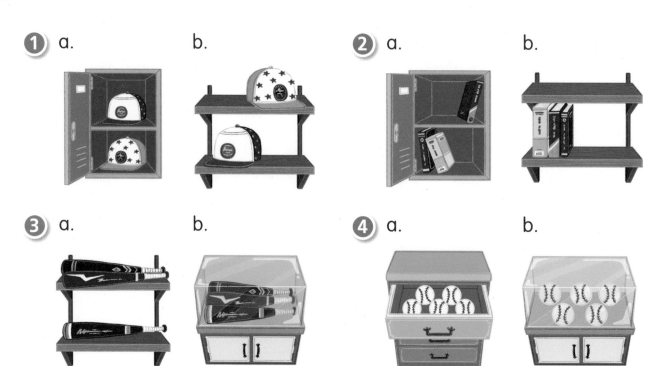

1 a.    b.

2 a.    b.

3 a.    b.

4 a.    b.

## C. Match, ask, and answer.

> A: Are they in the box?
> B: No, they are in the cabinet.

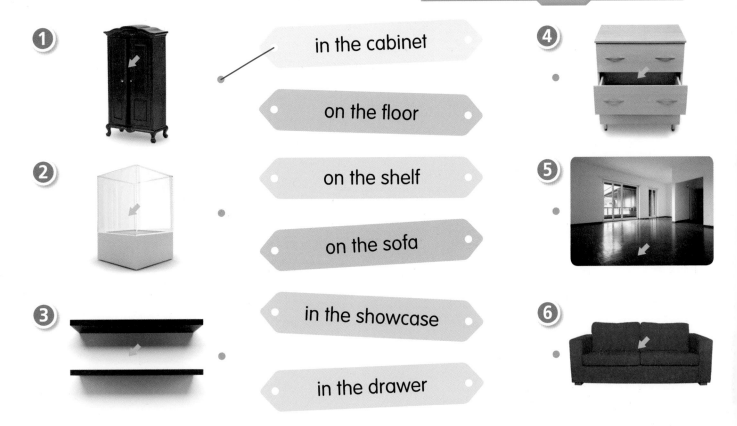

① in the cabinet

on the floor

② on the shelf

on the sofa

③ in the showcase

in the drawer

④

⑤

⑥

## D. Work with your friends.

- Place the things at the shop and talk with your friends.

bags

shoes

coats

hats

I'm looking for bags. Are they on the sofa?

No, they are on the shelf.

# Kero Got a New Bat!

**A. Listen and repeat.**

**B. Listen and number the pictures.**

38

C. Read and circle.

1. Kero is looking for ( bats, recorders ).

2. Kero is at a ( music store, sports shop ).

3. The bats are ( in the cabinet, on the shelf ).

D. Choose the things and do a role-play.

## A. Listen and sing.

**Let's Go to Buy One**

Oh, oh! I have to buy a recorder.

Okay. Okay. Let's go to buy one.

Where can I buy a recorder?

You can buy one at a music store.

What can I do for you?

I'm looking for recorders.

Are they on the shelf?

No! They are in the showcase.

## B. Play a board game.

★ A: Where can I buy a notebook?
B: You can buy one at a stationery store.

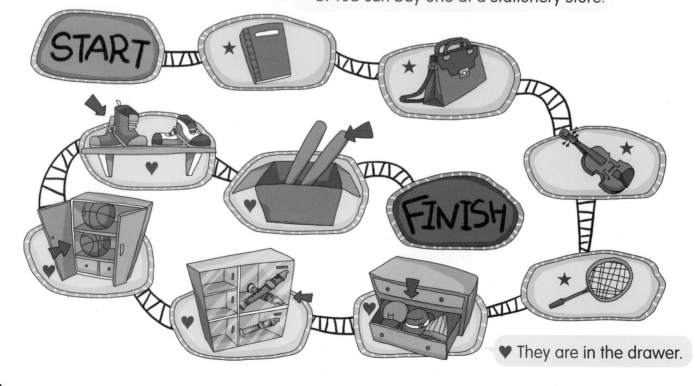

♥ They are in the drawer.

# Flea Markets

Flea markets are places where people go to sell or trade their goods. The goods are usually cheap and secondhand. Shopping at flea markets is a popular pastime for many people. The basic idea is to sell things you don't need. Flea markets are a good way to raise money. Let's take a look at the best items to sell at flea markets.

Clothes

Accessories

Old Books and Magazines

Old Furniture

## Check It Out!

1. What is the basic idea of flea markets?
2. What would you sell at flea markets?

# Assessment Test 1

**1. Listening**

## A. Listen and check.

**1**

a. ☐
b. ☐

**2**

a. ☐
b. ☐

**3**

a. ☐
b. ☐

**4**

a. ☐
b. ☐

**5**

a. ☐
b. ☐

**6**

a. ☐
b. ☐

## B. Listen and answer the questions.

**1** Which restaurant does Jenny want to go to?
a. She wants to go to an Italian restaurant.
b. She wants to go to a Chinese restaurant.
c. She wants to go to a Japanese restaurant.

**2** Where will they go?
a. a music store          b. a stationery store      c. a department store

## A. Look, listen, and reply.

**1**

**2**

**3**

**4**

## B. Number the sentences in order and talk with your partner.

( ) No, they are in the showcase.

( 1 ) What can I do for you?

( ) I'm looking for bats. Are they in the cabinet?

## A. Read and match.

1. Which restaurant do you want to go to?   •

2. Pass me a napkin, please.   •

3. Where can I buy a bat?   •

4. Are they in the box?   •

5. Are you ready to order?   •

6. How much is it?   •

• a. Yes, I am. I would like some spaghetti and meatballs.

• b. It is eighty dollars.

• c. No, they are in the cabinet.

• d. Sure.

• e. I want to go to an Italian restaurant.

• f. You can buy one at a sports shop.

## B. Read and check True or False.

Each country has its own food. Many Korean people eat out these days. What's your favorite food? Which restaurant do you want to go to? Look at some popular foods around the world. They look really delicious!

1. Curry from India
2. Sushi from Japan
3. Tacos from Mexico

1. Many Korean people eat out these days. .................. True ☐ False ☐

2. Curry is from Mexico. .................................... True ☐ False ☐

3. Sushi is from Japan. ..................................... True ☐ False ☐

e-learning

in the drawer    salad    ninety
music store    Chinese    salt    napkin

## A. Write the words.

**1**

**2**

**3**

**4**

_____      _____      _____      _____

**5**

**6**

**7**

They are _____.

Pass me a _____, please.

I would like a _____.

## B. Write the answers.

**1** Henry: Where can I buy a bat?
Mom: _____

( sports shop / can / you / buy / at / one / a /. )

**2** Henry: Are they in the box?
Clerk: No, _____.

( they / cabinet / in / are / the )

**3** Dad: Which restaurant do you want to go to?
Anna: _____

( want / Italian / to / restaurant / I / to / go / an /. )

## Lesson 11 At the Shop

Let's Talk

**A. Look, listen, and repeat.**

**Act It Out**

## B. Listen and practice.

I like the white one.

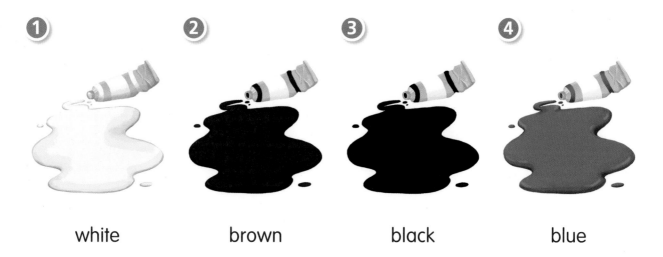

| ① | ② | ③ | ④ |
| white | brown | black | blue |

## C. Listen, point, and say.

A: Which one do you like?
B: I like the black one.

## Let's Learn

### A. Listen and chant.

There are so many hats.

Yes, you're right! Yes, you're right!

Hey, hey! Which one do you like?

White, white. I like the white one.

There are so many hats.

Yes, you're right! Yes, you're right!

Hey, hey! Which one do you like?

Brown, brown. I like the brown one.

### B. Read and choose.

ⓐ I like the brown one.　　ⓑ I like the white one.

ⓒ I like the black one.　　ⓓ I like the blue one.

## C. Match, ask, and answer.

A: Which one do you like?
B: I like the white one.

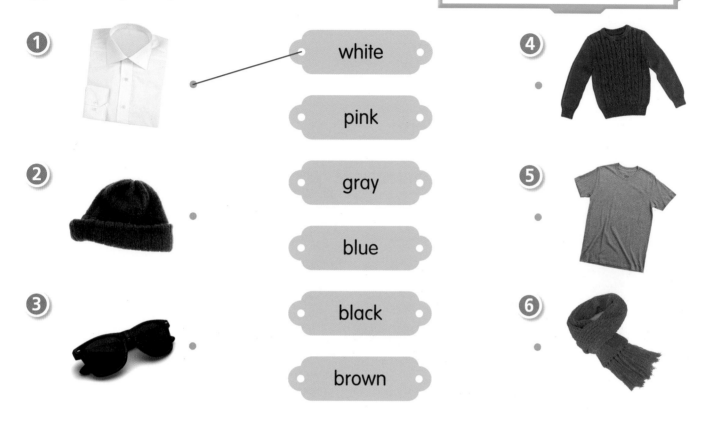

① white

pink

② gray

blue

③ black

brown

④

⑤

⑥

## D. Work with your friends.

- Ask your friends which one they like and write their names.

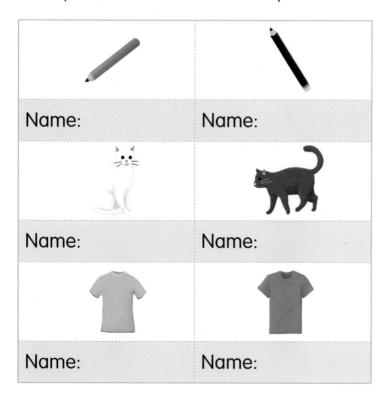

Name:          Name:

Name:          Name:

Name:          Name:

Which one do you like?

I like the orange one.

# Starting Times

**Let's Talk**

## A. Look, listen, and repeat.

It's this Sunday.

When is your baseball game?

It begins at twelve.

When does it begin?

It's this Sunday.

When is your concert?

When does it begin?

It begins at seven fifteen.

**ACT IT OUT**

It's this Sunday.

**B.** Listen and practice.

It begins at twelve.

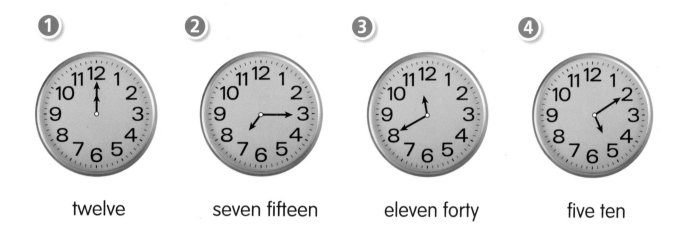

① twelve

② seven fifteen

③ eleven forty

④ five ten

**C.** Listen, point, and say.

A: When does it begin?
B: It begins at five ten.

Let's Learn

## A. Listen and chant.

When is your *baseball game*, your *baseball game*?

It's this Sunday. It's this Sunday!

When does it begin?

It begins at twelve! At twelve!

When is your *concert*, your *concert*?

It's this Sunday. It's this Sunday!

When does it begin?

It begins at *seven fifteen*! At *seven fifteen*!

## B. Listen and write.

①

It begins at _____ : _____.

②

It begins at _____ : _____.

③

It begins at _____ : _____.

④

It begins at _____ : _____.

## C. Ask, answer, and draw.

> A: When does it begin?
> B: It begins at twelve.

**①** twelve

**②** seven fifteen

**③** eleven forty

**④** five ten

**⑤** three thirty

**⑥** ten five

## D. Work with your friends.

- Make your own poster and talk with your friends.

Day:
Time:

Day:
Time:

When is your baseball game?

It's this Friday.

When does it begin?

It begins at twelve.

# My Baseball Game Begins at Twelve!

**A. Listen and repeat.**

**B. Listen and number the pictures.**

## C. Read and circle.

1. There are so many bats at a ( sports shop, music store ).
2. Kero  likes the ( brown, blue ) bat.
3. Kero's baseball game begins at ( twelve, three ).

## D. Choose the color you like and do a role-play.

## A. Listen and sing.

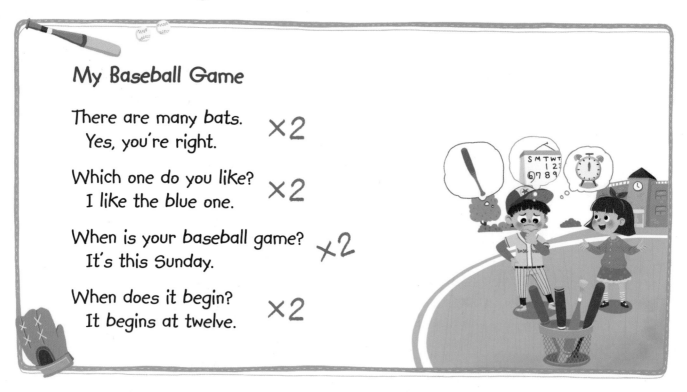

### My Baseball Game

There are many bats.
  Yes, you're right. ×2

Which one do you like?
  I like the blue one. ×2

When is your baseball game?
  It's this Sunday. ×2

When does it begin?
  It begins at twelve. ×2

## B. Play a board game.

START

★Which one do you like?

♥When does your baseball game begin?

5:10

Friday

♣When is your baseball game?

Back to Start

♥When does your concert begin?

●I like the _____ one.

★
Which one do you like?

●I like the _____ one.

FINISH

e-learning

# Earth Hour

Earth Hour is a global event to save the Earth. It is held on the last Saturday in March. People turn off their lights for an hour from 8:30 p.m. to 9:30 p.m. Earth Hour started in Sydney, Australia, in 2007. Now, it is held all around the world. People in more than 7,000 cities and towns turn off their lights on this day.

**Check It Out!**

1. What is Earth Hour?
2. What do we do during Earth Hour?

## Let's Talk

### A. Look, listen, and repeat.

## B. Listen and practice.

I have to cook dinner.

① cook dinner

② go to the animal hospital

③ do the laundry

④ water the flowers

## C. Listen, point, and say.

A: Why are you busy?
B: I have to do the laundry.

## Let's Learn

### A. Listen and chant.

Let's, let's, let's play the recorder together.

Sorry, sorry, sorry. I'm busy.

Why are you busy?

I have to cook dinner.

Let's, let's, let's play baseball together.

Sorry, sorry, sorry. I'm busy.

Why are you busy?

I have to go to the animal hospital.

### B. Listen and number.

ⓐ  ◯

ⓑ  ◯

ⓒ  ◯

ⓓ  ◯

## C. Ask and answer.

> A: Why are you busy?
> B: I have to cook dinner.

① cook dinner

② go to the animal hospital

③ do the laundry

④ water the flowers

⑤ wash the dishes

⑥ fix the roof

## D. Work with your friends.

- Draw what you have to do now. And tell the reason why you can't play outside.

Let's play outside.

Sorry. I have to do my homework.

Reasons

☐ do my homework
☐ wash the dishes
☐ help my mom
☐ clean my room

## Lesson 15 Making Suggestions

### A. Look, listen, and repeat.

It's raining, Henry.

Oh, no. We can't play baseball.

Let's play baseball at the gym.

Sounds great.

Oh, look. It's sunny now.

Oh, you're right.

Let's play baseball on the playground.

Sounds good.

**ACT IT OUT**

Oh, no. We can't play baseball.

## B. Listen and practice.

Let's play baseball at the gym.

1 at the gym

2 at the indoor stadium

3 on the playground

4 in the backyard

A: Let's play baseball at the gym.
B: Sounds great.

## C. Listen, point, and say.

## A. Listen and chant.

Let's play *baseball* on the playground!
On the playground!
   Sounds good! Sounds good!
It's raining! It's raining!
   Oh, no! Oh, no!
   We can't play *baseball*.
   We can't play *baseball*!
It's sunny now! It's sunny now!
Let's play *baseball*, *baseball*!
   Sounds great! Sounds great!

## B. Read and choose.

① ② ③ ④

ⓐ Let's play basketball on the playground.

ⓑ Let's play basketball at the gym.

ⓒ Let's play basketball in the backyard.

ⓓ Let's play basketball at the indoor stadium.

## C. Go down the ladder. Then, ask and answer.

A: Let's play baseball at the gym.
B: Sounds great.

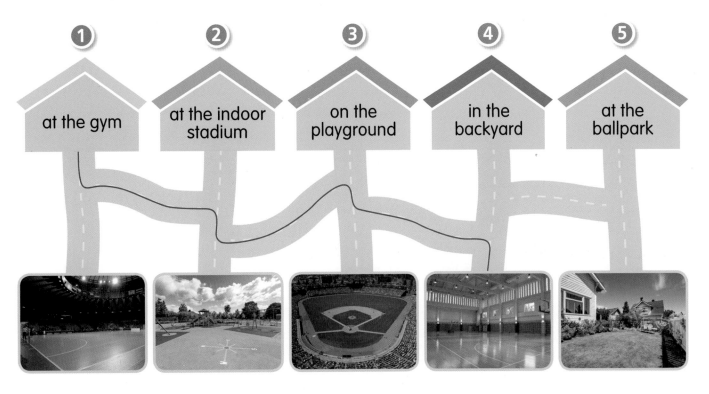

① at the gym
② at the indoor stadium
③ on the playground
④ in the backyard
⑤ at the ballpark

## D. Work with your friends.

- Think, draw, and talk with your friends.

Oh, no! We can't swim in the river.

Solution → ... at the swimming pool.

Oh, no! We can't play soccer.

Let's play soccer in the backyard.

Solution

# Playing Badminton on a Rainy Day

## A. Listen and repeat.

## B. Listen and number the pictures.

... cook dinner.

## C. Read and answer the questions.

**1** What does Kero want to play?    a. badminton      b. baseball

**2** Why is Kero's mom busy?    a. to do the laundry    b. to cook dinner

**3** Where can Kero play badminton?    a. on the playground    b. at the gym

## D. Choose a sport you want to play with your friend and do a role-play.

## A. Listen and sing.

Let's Play Badminton

Let's play badminton together, together.
　Sorry, sorry. I'm busy.
Why? Why? Why are you busy?
　I have to go to the animal hospital.
Oh, no.

Let's play badminton together, together.
　Look, look. It's raining.
Oh, no. We can't play badminton.
　Let's play badminton at the gym.
Sounds good.

## B. Play a board game.

♣ I have to cook dinner.

● Let's play baseball at the gym.

# Let's Help the Children

We are busy because we go to school and do our homework. However, some children in poor countries don't go to school. Instead, they work all day long because they have to earn money. Many of them are hungry and sick. Let's help the children in poor countries.

## Check It Out!

1. Some children in poor countries don't go to school. Why not?
2. How can we help the children in poor countries?

# Your Baseball Position

**Let's Talk**

## A. Look, listen, and repeat.

What's your position?

I'm a catcher.

Are you a catcher, too?

No, I'm not. I'm an umpire.

What's your position?

I'm a pitcher.

Are you a pitcher, too?

No, I'm not. I'm a hitter.

**ACT IT OUT**

What's your position?

**B.** **Listen and practice.**

Are you a catcher, too?

① catcher   ② umpire   ③ pitcher   ④ hitter

A: Are you a hitter, too?
B: No, I'm not. I'm a pitcher.

**C.** **Listen, point, and say.**

## A. Listen and chant.

What's your position?

  Catcher. I'm a catcher.

  Are you a catcher, too?

No, I'm not.

Umpire. I'm an umpire.

What's your position?

  Pitcher. I'm a pitcher.

Are you a pitcher, too?

  No, I'm not.

  Hitter. I'm a hitter.

## B. Read and choose.

ⓐ I'm an umpire.

ⓑ I'm a catcher.

ⓒ I'm a hitter.

ⓓ I'm a pitcher.

## C. Match, ask, and answer.

> A: Are you a hitter, too?
> B: No, I'm not. I'm a catcher.

① catcher  ② umpire  ③ pitcher  ④ hitter  ⑤ coach  ⑥ cheerleader

## D. Work with your friends.

- Ask your friends and write their names on the positions.

Name:

Name:

Name:

Name:

No, I'm not. I'm a catcher.

Jenny, are you a pitcher, too?

# Lesson 18

# Does He Play Ice Hockey?

## A. Look, listen, and repeat.

Who is she?

She's my friend Kelly.

Does she play baseball?

Yes, she does.

He's my friend Danny.

Does he play ice hockey?

Who is he?

No, he doesn't.

**Act It Out**

Who is she?

74

## B. Listen and practice.

Does he play ice hockey?

① play ice hockey   ② play table tennis   ③ play golf   ④ go bowling

## C. Listen, point, and say.

A: Does he play ice hockey?
B: Yes, he does.

## A. Listen and chant.

Who is she?

She's my friend Kelly.

Does she play baseball?          Who is he?

Does she play baseball?          He's my friend Sam.

Yes, she does.                   Does he play ice hockey?

Yes, she does.                   Does he play ice hockey?

Yes, he does.

Yes, he does.

## B. Listen and check.

**1** True ☐  False ☐

**2** True ☐  False ☐

**3** True ☐  False ☐

**4** True ☐  False ☐

e-learning

## C. Ask and answer.

> A: Does he play ice hockey?
> B: Yes, he does.

**①**
play ice hockey

**②**
play table tennis

**③**
play golf

**④**
go bowling

**⑤**
play baseball

**⑥**
do taegwondo

## D. Work with your friends.

- What sports do your family members play? Ask and write the sports names.

Does your dad play golf?

Yes, he does.

☐ play golf
☐ play badminton
☐ go swimming
☐ do yoga

|  | Grandpa | Grandma | Dad | Mom | Sister | Brother |
|---|---|---|---|---|---|---|
| You |  |  |  |  |  |  |
| Your Friend |  |  |  |  |  |  |

# Kero Is a Pitcher!

**A.** Listen and repeat.

**B.** Listen and number the pictures.

## C. Read and check True or False.

1 Kero  is a pitcher. .................................... True ☐ False ☐

2 Mr. Smith is a catcher. .................................... True ☐ False ☐

3 Mr. Smith plays baseball every day. .................................... True ☐ False ☐

## D. Choose the position you want to play in the baseball game and do a role-play.

 ☐       ☐

## A. Listen and sing.

**I'm a Pitcher**

I am an umpire. What's your position?

  I am a pitcher. I am a pitcher.

Are you a pitcher, too? Are you a pitcher, too?

  No, I'm not. I am a catcher.

Who is he? Who is he?

  He's my friend Timmy.

Does he play *baseball*?

  Yes, he does. He is a hitter. He is a hitter.

## B. Play a board game.

Are you a catcher, too?

Does he play ice hockey?

Does she play table tennis?

What's your position?

Start

Does he go bowling?

Does he play golf?

What's your position?

Finish

Are you a pitcher, too?

e-learning

# Baseball Positions

A baseball team has nine players. All of them have their own positions. The pitcher stands on the mound, and he throws the balls. The catcher gives signs to the pitcher.

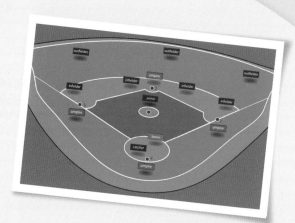

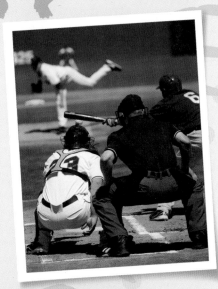

When the hitter misses the ball, the catcher catches it. The 1st, 2nd, and 3rd basemen play on their bases. The shortstop stands between the 2nd and 3rd basemen. There are three outfielders to cover the outfield.

## Check It Out!

1. How many players are there on a team?
2. What does a catcher do?

## 1. Listening

**A. Listen and check.**

**①**

a. ☐
b. ☐

**②**

a. ☐
b. ☐

**③**

a. ☐
b. ☐

**④**

a. ☐
b. ☐

**⑤**

a. ☐
b. ☐

**⑥**

a. ☐
b. ☐

**B. Listen and answer the questions.**

**①** What does Jack want to do with Julie?
a. He wants to play baseball.
b. He wants to play basketball.
c. He wants to go to the animal hospital.

**②** What is Tom's position?
a. a catcher          b. a pitcher          c. an umpire

## 2. Speaking

### A. Look, listen, and reply.

### B. Number the sentences in order and talk with your partner.

◯ Sorry. I'm busy.

① Let's play badminton at the gym.

◯ Why are you busy?

◯ I have to cook dinner.

## A. Read and match.

1. Let's play baseball on the playground.  •

2. Who is he?  •

3. Why are you busy?  •

4. Are you a pitcher, too?  •

5. Which one do you like?  •

6. When does it begin?  •

• a. I have to cook dinner.

• b. Sounds good.

• c. He's my friend Jake.

• d. I like the brown one.

• e. It begins at five ten.

• f. No, I'm not. I'm a hitter.

## B. Read and check True or False.

Peter: Wow! There are so many recorders!
Sally: Yes, you're right!
Peter: Which one do you like?
Sally: I like the brown one.
Peter: When is your concert?
Sally: It's this Sunday.
Peter: When does it begin?
Sally: It begins at twelve. Will you come?
Peter: Sorry. I can't. I have a baseball game at eleven forty on that day.

1. Sally likes the brown recorder. .................................. True ☐  False ☐

2. Sally has a concert this Sunday. .................................. True ☐  False ☐

3. Peter's baseball game begins at twelve this Sunday. ... True ☐  False ☐

e-learning

at the indoor stadium    pitcher    eleven forty
cook dinner    go bowling    white    hitter

## A. Write the words.

**1**

**2**

**3**

**4**

_____    _____    _____    _____

**5**

**6**

**7**

Does he _____ ?      It begins at _____ .      I am a _____ .

## B. Write the answers.

**1**  Mom: Which one do you like?
Henry: _____
( the / I / one / brown / like /. )

**2**  Mom: When does your baseball game begin?
Henry: _____
( at / twelve / begins / it /. )

**3**  Henry: Why are you busy?
Mom: _____
( dinner / I / cook / to / have /. )

# Syllabus

| | Topic | Language | Key Vocabulary |
|---|---|---|---|
| **Lesson 1** | Choosing a Restaurant | Which restaurant do you want to go to?<br>- I want to go to an Italian restaurant.<br>Let's eat out.<br>- Okay. | Italian<br>Chinese<br>Indian<br>Japanese |
| **Lesson 2** | At the Restaurant | I would like a salad.<br>- Okay.<br>Are you ready to order?<br>- Yes, I am. | salad<br>spaghetti and meatballs<br>potato pizza<br>garlic bread |
| **Lesson 3** | Kero Is at an Italian Restaurant | Step Up 1 (Review Lessons 1-2)<br>*Reading Time: The World's Popular Foods | |
| **Lesson 4** | Table Manners | Pass me the salt, please. - Sure.<br>Don't speak with your mouth full. - Okay.<br>Cover your mouth when you cough.<br>- Okay. | salt<br>napkin<br>sugar<br>pepper |
| **Lesson 5** | Asking about Prices | How much is it?<br>- It is eighty dollars.<br>How was the food?<br>- It was delicious. | eighty<br>ninety<br>one hundred<br>one hundred twenty |
| **Lesson 6** | Don't Speak with Your Mouth Full | Step Up 2 (Review Lessons 4-5)<br>*Reading Time: Table Manners | |
| **Lesson 7** | Places to Buy Things | Where can I buy a recorder?<br>- You can buy one at a music store.<br>Oh, I have to buy a recorder.<br>- Okay, let's go to buy one. | music store<br>sports shop<br>department store<br>stationery store |
| **Lesson 8** | Places to Find | Are they in the cabinet?<br>- No, they are in the showcase.<br>What can I do for you?<br>- I'm looking for recorders. | in the cabinet<br>in the showcase<br>on the shelf<br>in the drawer |
| **Lesson 9** | Kero Got a New Bat! | Step Up 3 (Review Lessons 7-8)<br>*Reading Time: Flea Markets | |
| **Lesson 10** | Assessment Test 1 (Review Lessons 1-9) | | |

| | Topic | Language | Key Vocabulary |
|---|---|---|---|
| **Lesson 11** | At the Shop | Which one do you like?<br>- I like the white one.<br>There are so many recorders.<br>- Yes, you're right. | white<br>brown<br>black<br>blue |
| **Lesson 12** | Starting Times | When does it begin?<br>- It begins at twelve.<br>When is your baseball game?<br>- It's this Sunday. | twelve<br>seven fifteen<br>eleven forty<br>five ten |
| **Lesson 13** | My Baseball Game Begins at Twelve! | Step Up 4 ( Review Lessons  11-12)<br>*Reading Time: Earth Hour | |
| **Lesson 14** | Asking for Reasons | Why are you busy?<br>- I have to cook dinner.<br>Let's play the recorder together.<br>- Sorry. I'm busy. | cook dinner<br>go to the animal hospital<br>do the laundry<br>water the flowers |
| **Lesson 15** | Making Suggestions | Let's play baseball at the gym.<br>- Sounds great.<br>It's raining, Henry.<br>- Oh, no. We can't play baseball. | at the gym<br>at the indoor stadium<br>on the playground<br>in the backyard |
| **Lesson 16** | Playing Badminton on a Rainy Day | Step Up 5 (Review Lessons 14-15)<br>*Reading Time: Let's Help the Children | |
| **Lesson 17** | Your Baseball Position | Are you a catcher, too?<br>- No, I'm not. I'm an umpire.<br>What's your position?<br>- I'm a catcher. | catcher<br>umpire<br>pitcher<br>hitter |
| **Lesson 18** | Does He Play Ice Hockey? | Does he play ice hockey?<br>- Yes, he does.<br>Who is she?<br>- She is my friend Kelly. | play ice hockey<br>play table tennis<br>play golf<br>go bowling |
| **Lesson 19** | Kero Is a Pitcher! | Step Up 6 (Review Lessons 17-18)<br>*Reading Time: Baseball Positions | |
| **Lesson 20** | Assessment Test 2 (Review Lessons 11-19) | | |

| | | | | | |
|---|---|---|---|---|---|
| | Italian | | Chinese | | Indian |
| | Japanese | | salad | | spaghetti and meatballs |
| | potato pizza | | garlic bread | | salt |
| | napkin | | sugar | | pepper |
| | eighty | | ninety | | one hundred |
| | one hundred twenty | | music store | | sports shop |
| | department store | | stationery store | | in the cabinet |
| | in the showcase | | on the shelf | | in the drawer |
| | white | | brown | | black |
| | blue | | twelve | | seven fifteen |
| | eleven forty | | five ten | | cook dinner |
| | go to the animal hospital | | do the laundry | | water the flowers |
| | at the gym | | at the indoor stadium | | on the playground |
| | in the backyard | | catcher | | umpire |
| | pitcher | | hitter | | play ice hockey |
| | play table tennis | | play golf | | go bowling |

## Lesson 1   Choosing a Restaurant

| | Vocabulary | Meaning | Sentence |
|---|---|---|---|
| 1 | Italian* | 이탈리아의 | I want to go to an Italian restaurant. |
| 2 | Chinese* | 중국의 | I want to go to a Chinese restaurant. |
| 3 | Indian* | 인도의 | I want to go to an Indian restaurant. |
| 4 | Japanese* | 일본의 | I want to go to a Japanese restaurant. |
| 5 | Korean* | 한국의 | I want to go to a Korean restaurant. |
| 6 | Mexican* | 멕시코의 | I want to go to a Mexican restaurant. |
| 7 | eat | 먹다 | Let's eat out. |
| 8 | out | 밖으로 | Let's eat out. |
| 9 | which | 어떤, 어느 | Which restaurant do you want to go to? |
| 10 | restaurant | 레스토랑, 식당 | Which restaurant do you want to go to? |
| 11 | want | 원하다 | Which restaurant do you want to go to? |
| 12 | sure | 그래(요) | Sure, let's go. |

## Lesson 2   At the Restaurant

| | Vocabulary | Meaning | Sentence |
|---|---|---|---|
| 1 | salad* | 샐러드 | I would like a salad. |
| 2 | spaghetti and meatballs* | 스파게티와 미트볼 | I would like some spaghetti and meatballs. |
| 3 | potato pizza* | 감자 피자 | I would like some potato pizza. |
| 4 | garlic bread* | 마늘빵 | I would like some garlic bread. |
| 5 | sandwiches* | sandwich(샌드위치)의 복수형 | I would like some sandwiches. |
| 6 | curry* | 카레(요리) | I would like some curry. |
| 7 | ready | 준비가 된 | Are you ready to order? |
| 8 | order | 주문하다 | Are you ready to order? |
| 9 | yes | 그래(요) | Yes, I am. |
| 10 | would like | ~하고 싶다 | I would like a salad. |
| 11 | some | 조금, 약간의 | I would like some spaghetti and meatballs. |
| 12 | yeah | [감탄사] 응, 그래 | Yeah! |

## Lesson 5   Asking about Prices

| | Vocabulary | Meaning | Sentence |
|---|---|---|---|
| 1 | eighty* | 80 | It is eighty dollars. |
| 2 | ninety* | 90 | It is ninety dollars. |
| 3 | one hundred* | 100 | It is one hundred dollars. |
| 4 | one hundred twenty* | 120 | It is one hundred twenty dollars. |
| 5 | sixty* | 60 | It is sixty dollars. |
| 6 | seventy* | 70 | It is seventy dollars. |
| 7 | how | 어떻게 | How was the food? |
| 8 | food | 음식 | How was the food? |
| 9 | delicious | 맛있는 | It was delicious. |
| 10 | how much | (양·값이) 얼마, 어느 정도 | How much is it? |
| 11 | dollar | 달러 (화폐 단위) | It is eighty dollars. |
| 12 | good | 좋은 | It was good. |

## Lesson 6   Don't Speak with Your Mouth Full

| | Vocabulary | Meaning | Sentence |
|---|---|---|---|
| 1 | common | 흔한, 보통의 | There are some common table manners when you have food. |
| 2 | manner | 태도, 예의 | There are some common table manners when you have food. |
| 3 | mouth | 입 | Don't speak with your mouth full. |
| 4 | difference | 차이 | There are some differences between countries. |
| 5 | rude | 무례한 | It is very rude to burp during a meal. |
| 6 | burp | 트림하다 | It is very rude to burp during a meal. |
| 7 | during a meal | 식사 중에 | It is very rude to burp during a meal. |
| 8 | blow one's nose | ~의 코를 풀다 | Don't blow your nose. |
| 9 | complain | 불평하다 | Don't complain about the food. |
| 10 | bring | 가져오다 | Bring your dishes to the sink. |
| 11 | sink | 싱크대 | Bring your dishes to the sink. |
| 12 | other | 다른 | What other table manners do you know? |

## Lesson 3 — Kero Is at an Italian Restaurant

| | Vocabulary | Meaning | Sentence |
|---|---|---|---|
| 1 | each | 각각의 | Each country has its own food. |
| 2 | country | 나라 | Each country has its own food. |
| 3 | own | 자신의 | Each country has its own food. |
| 4 | Korean | 한국(사람)의 | Many Korean people eat out these days. |
| 5 | people | 사람들 | Many Korean people eat out these days. |
| 6 | eat out | 외식하다 | Many Korean people eat out these days. |
| 7 | these days | 요즘에는 | Many Korean people eat out these days. |
| 8 | popular | 유명한 | Look at some popular foods around the world. |
| 9 | really | 정말로 | They look really delicious! |
| 10 | Japan | 일본 | Sushi from Japan |
| 11 | Italy | 이탈리아 | Napoli Pizza from Italy |
| 12 | Mexico | 멕시코 | Tacos from Mexico |

## Lesson 4 — Table Manners

| | Vocabulary | Meaning | Sentence |
|---|---|---|---|
| 1 | salt* | 소금 | Pass me the salt, please. |
| 2 | napkin* | 냅킨 | Pass me a napkin, please. |
| 3 | sugar* | 설탕 | Pass me the sugar, please. |
| 4 | pepper* | 후추 | Pass me the pepper, please. |
| 5 | bowl* | (우묵한) 그릇 | Pass me a bowl, please. |
| 6 | fork* | 포크 | Pass me a fork, please. |
| 7 | speak | 말하다 | Don't speak with your mouth full. |
| 8 | full | 가득한 | Don't speak with your mouth full. |
| 9 | pass | 건네주다 | Pass me the salt, please. |
| 10 | cover | 가리다 | Cover your mouth when you cough. |
| 11 | when | ~할 때 | Cover your mouth when you cough. |
| 12 | cough | 기침하다 | Cover your mouth when you cough. |

## Lesson 7 — Places to Buy Things

| | Vocabulary | Meaning | Sentence |
|---|---|---|---|
| 1 | music store* | 악기점 | You can buy one at a music store. |
| 2 | sports shop* | 스포츠 용품점 | You can buy one at a sports shop. |
| 3 | department store* | 백화점 | You can buy one at a department store. |
| 4 | stationery store* | 문구점 | You can buy one at a stationery store. |
| 5 | drugstore* | 약국 | You can buy one at a drugstore. |
| 6 | pet shop* | 애완 동물 용품점 | You can buy one at a pet shop. |
| 7 | have to | ~해야 한다 | Oh, I have to buy a recorder. |
| 8 | buy | 사다 | I have to buy a recorder. |
| 9 | recorder | 리코더 | I have to buy a recorder. |
| 10 | where | 어디에 | Where can I buy a recorder? |
| 11 | at | (장소) ~에서 | You can buy one at a music store. |
| 12 | bat | 야구 방망이 | Oh, I have to buy a bat. |

## Lesson 8 — Places to Find

| | Vocabulary | Meaning | Sentence |
|---|---|---|---|
| 1 | in the cabinet* | 캐비닛 안에 | Are they in the cabinet? |
| 2 | in the showcase* | 진열장 안에 | No, they are in the showcase. |
| 3 | on the shelf* | 선반 위에 | No, they are on the shelf. |
| 4 | in the drawer* | 서랍 안에 | No, they are in the drawer. |
| 5 | on the floor* | 바닥 위에 | No, they are on the floor. |
| 6 | on the sofa* | 소파 위에 | No, they are on the sofa. |
| 7 | what | 무엇 | What can I do for you? |
| 8 | can | ~할 수 있다 | What can I do for you? |
| 9 | do | 하다 | What can I do for you? |
| 10 | for | ~을 위해 | What can I do for you? |
| 11 | look for | 찾다 | I'm looking for recorders. |
| 12 | in the box | 상자 안에 | Are they in the box? |

## Lesson 9 — Kero Got a New Bat!

| | Vocabulary | Meaning | Sentence |
|---|---|---|---|
| 1 | flea market | 벼룩시장 | Flea markets are places where people go to sell or trade their goods. |
| 2 | sell | 팔다 | Flea markets are places where people go to sell or trade their goods. |
| 3 | trade | 무역하다 | Flea markets are places where people go to sell or trade their goods. |
| 4 | usually | 대개, 보통 | The goods are usually cheap and secondhand. |
| 5 | cheap | 값이 싼 | The goods are usually cheap and secondhand. |
| 6 | secondhand | 중고의 | The goods are usually cheap and secondhand. |
| 7 | pastime | 취미 | Shopping at flea markets is a popular pastime for many people. |
| 8 | basic | 기본의, 기초의 | The basic idea is to sell things you don't need. |
| 9 | best | 최고의 | Let's take a look at the best items to sell. |
| 10 | item | 품목 | Let's take a look at the best items to sell. |
| 11 | magazine | 잡지 | You can sell old magazines. |
| 12 | furniture | 가구 | You can sell old furniture. |

## Lesson 11 — At the Shop

| | Vocabulary | Meaning | Sentence |
|---|---|---|---|
| 1 | white* | 흰색의 | I like the white one. |
| 2 | brown* | 갈색의 | I like the brown one. |
| 3 | black* | 검은 | I like the black one. |
| 4 | blue* | 파란 | I like the blue one. |
| 5 | gray* | 회색의 | I like the gray one. |
| 6 | pink* | 분홍색의 | I like the pink one. |
| 7 | there are | ~이 있다 | There are so many recorders. |
| 8 | so | 매우 | There are so many recorders. |
| 9 | many | 많은 | There are so many recorders. |
| 10 | right | 옳은 | Yes, you're right. |
| 11 | which one | 어느 것 | Which one do you like? |
| 12 | like | 좋아하다 | Which one do you like? |

## Lesson 14 — Asking for Reasons

| | Vocabulary | Meaning | Sentence |
|---|---|---|---|
| 1 | cook dinner* | 저녁 식사를 준비하다 | I have to cook dinner. |
| 2 | go to the animal hospital* | 동물 병원에 가다 | I have to go to the animal hospital. |
| 3 | do the laundry* | 빨래를 하다 | I have to do the laundry. |
| 4 | water the flowers* | 꽃에 물을 주다 | I have to water the flowers. |
| 5 | wash the dishes* | 설거지를 하다 | I have to wash the dishes. |
| 6 | fix the roof* | 지붕을 수리하다 | I have to fix the roof. |
| 7 | play | 연주하다 | Let's play the recorder together. |
| 8 | together | 함께 | Let's play the recorder together. |
| 9 | sorry | 미안해 | Sorry. |
| 10 | busy | 바쁜 | I'm busy. |
| 11 | why | 왜, 어째서 | Why are you busy? |
| 12 | play baseball | 야구를 하다 | Let's play baseball together. |

## Lesson 15 — Making Suggestions

| | Vocabulary | Meaning | Sentence |
|---|---|---|---|
| 1 | at the gym* | 체육관에서 | Let's play baseball at the gym. |
| 2 | at the indoor stadium* | 실내 경기장에서 | Let's play baseball at the indoor stadium. |
| 3 | on the playground* | 놀이터에서 | Let's play baseball on the playground. |
| 4 | in the backyard* | 뒷마당에서 | Let's play baseball in the backyard. |
| 5 | at the ballpark* | 야구장에서 | Let's play baseball at the ballpark. |
| 6 | rain | 비가 오다 | It's raining. |
| 7 | can't | ~할 수 없다 (cannot의 축약형) | We can't play baseball. |
| 8 | look | 보다 | Oh, look. |
| 9 | sunny | 화창한 | It's sunny now. |
| 10 | now | 지금 | It's sunny now. |
| 11 | swim | 수영하다 | We can't swim in the river. |
| 12 | play soccer | 축구를 하다 | Let's play soccer in the backyard. |

## Lesson 12 — Starting Times

| | Vocabulary | Meaning | Sentence |
|---|---|---|---|
| 1 | twelve* | 12시 | It begins at twelve. |
| 2 | seven fifteen* | 7시 15분 | It begins at seven fifteen. |
| 3 | eleven forty* | 11시 40분 | It begins at eleven forty. |
| 4 | five ten* | 5시 10분 | It begins at five ten. |
| 5 | three thirty* | 3시 30분 | It begins at three thirty. |
| 6 | ten five* | 10시 5분 | It begins at ten five. |
| 7 | when | 언제 | When is your baseball game? |
| 8 | baseball game | 야구 경기 | When is your baseball game? |
| 9 | Sunday | 일요일 | It's this Sunday. |
| 10 | begin | 시작하다 | When does it begin? |
| 11 | at | (시간) ~에 | It begins at twelve. |
| 12 | concert | 콘서트 | When is your concert? |

## Lesson 13 — My Baseball Game Begins at Twelve!

| | Vocabulary | Meaning | Sentence |
|---|---|---|---|
| 1 | use | 사용하다 | I'll use it in my baseball game. |
| 2 | know | 알다 | I know. |
| 3 | Earth | 지구 | Earth Hour is a global event to save the Earth. |
| 4 | event | 행사 | Earth Hour is a global event to save the Earth. |
| 5 | save | 구하다 | Earth Hour is a global event to save the Earth. |
| 6 | be held | 열리다 | It is held on the last Saturday in March. |
| 7 | last | 마지막 | It is held on the last Saturday in March. |
| 8 | March | 3월 | It is held on the last Saturday in March. |
| 9 | turn off | (불, 전기 등을) 끄다 | People turn off their lights for an hour. |
| 10 | light | (전)등 | People turn off their lights for an hour. |
| 11 | for an hour | 한 시간 동안 | People turn off their lights for an hour. |
| 12 | city | 도시 | People in more than 7,000 cities turn off their lights on this day. |

## Lesson 16 — Playing Badminton on a Rainy Day

| | Vocabulary | Meaning | Sentence |
|---|---|---|---|
| 1 | play badminton | 배드민턴을 하다 | Let's play badminton, Mom. |
| 2 | want | 원하다 | What does Kero want to play? |
| 3 | it | 시간, 날짜, 날씨 등을 나타내는 비인칭 주어 | It's raining. |
| 4 | help | 돕다 | Let's help the children. |
| 5 | go to school | 학교에 가다 | We are busy because we go to school. |
| 6 | do one's homework | ~의 숙제를 하다 | We are busy because we do our homework. |
| 7 | however | 그러나 | However, some children in poor countries don't go to school. |
| 8 | poor | 가난한 | Some children in poor countries don't go to school. |
| 9 | instead | 대신에 | Instead, they work all day long. |
| 10 | all day long | 하루 종일 | Instead, they work all day long. |
| 11 | earn money | 돈을 벌다 | Because they have to earn money. |
| 12 | hungry | 배고픈 | Many of them are hungry and sick. |

## Lesson 17 — Your Baseball Position

| | Vocabulary | Meaning | Sentence |
|---|---|---|---|
| 1 | catcher* | 포수 | I'm a catcher. |
| 2 | umpire* | 심판 | I'm an umpire. |
| 3 | pitcher* | 투수 | I'm a pitcher. |
| 4 | hitter* | 타자 | I'm a hitter. |
| 5 | coach* | 코치, 지도자 | I'm a coach. |
| 6 | cheerleader* | 치어리더 | I'm a cheerleader. |
| 7 | what's | 무엇입니까 (what is의 축약형) | What's your position? |
| 8 | your | 너의 | What's your position? |
| 9 | position | 위치 | What's your position? |
| 10 | I | 나는 | I'm a catcher. |
| 11 | too | 또한, 역시 | Are you a catcher, too? |
| 12 | not | ~아니다 | No, I'm not. |

## Lesson 18 — Does He Play Ice Hockey?

| | Vocabulary | Meaning | Sentence |
|---|---|---|---|
| 1 | play ice hockey* | 아이스하키를 하다 | Does he play ice hockey? |
| 2 | play table tennis* | 탁구를 치다 | Does he play table tennis? |
| 3 | play golf* | 골프를 치다 | Does he play golf? |
| 4 | go bowling* | 볼링을 치다 | Does he go bowling? |
| 5 | play baseball* | 야구를 하다 | Does he play baseball? |
| 6 | do taegwondo* | 태권도를 하다 | Does he do taegwondo? |
| 7 | who | 누구 | Who is she? |
| 8 | she | 그녀 | Who is she? |
| 9 | my | 나의 | She's my friend Kelly. |
| 10 | friend | 친구 | She's my friend Kelly. |
| 11 | does | do의 3인칭 단수 현재형 | Does she play baseball? |
| 12 | he | 그 | Who is he? |

## Lesson 19 — Kero Is a Pitcher!

| | Vocabulary | Meaning | Sentence |
|---|---|---|---|
| 1 | teacher | 선생님 | He is my teacher Mr. Smith. |
| 2 | Mr. | 남자의 성, 성명 앞에 붙임 ~ 씨[님, 선생] | He is my teacher Mr. Smith. |
| 3 | every day | 매일 | Does he play baseball every day? |
| 4 | good luck | 행운 | Good luck! |
| 5 | stand on | ~위에 서다 | The pitcher stands on the mound. |
| 6 | mound | 흙더미, 마운드 | The pitcher stands on the mound. |
| 7 | throw | 던지다 | The pitcher throws the balls. |
| 8 | give signs | 신호들을 보내다 | The catcher gives signs to the pitcher. |
| 9 | miss | 놓치다 | When the hitter misses the ball, the catcher catches it. |
| 10 | catch | 잡다 | When the hitter misses the ball, the catcher catches it. |
| 11 | outfielder | (야구) 외야수 | There are three outfielders to cover the outfield. |
| 12 | outfield | (야구) 외야 | There are three outfielders to cover the outfield. |

 **Memo**

 **Memo**

# Answers

# Student Book
# Answers

## Lesson 1 Choosing a Restaurant
**B. Read and write the numbers.** p. 8

**C. Match, ask, and answer.** p. 9

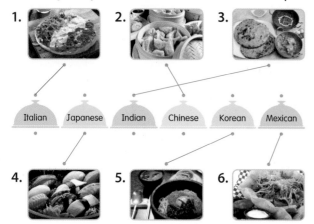

## Lesson 2 At the Restaurant
**B. Listen and match.** p. 12

**2.** ⓐ   **3.** ⓑ   **4.** ⓓ

**C. Go down the ladder. Then, ask and answer.**
p. 13

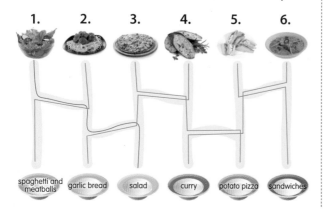

## Lesson 3 Kero Is at an Italian Restaurant
**B. Listen and number the pictures.** p. 14

**C. Read and circle.** p. 15

- Kero 😼 wants to go to ( an Italian, (a Chinese) ) restaurant.

- Kiki 🐶 wants to go to ( (an Italian), a Chinese ) restaurant.

**Reading Time** p. 17

**1.** Sushi comes from Japan.

**2.** [Example] I want to go to a French restaurant for lunch.

## Lesson 4 Table Manners
**B. Listen and number.** p. 20

**a.** 4   **b.** 1   **c.** 3   **d.** 2

**C. Match, ask, and answer.** p. 21

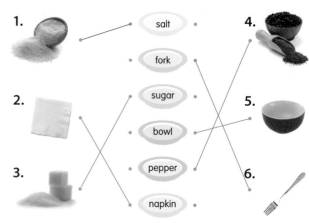

## Lesson 5 Asking about Prices
**B. Look, read, and write the prices.** p. 24

**2.** 100   **3.** 90   **4.** 120

## C. Match, ask, and answer. p. 25

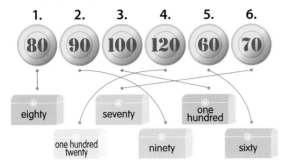

## Lesson 6 Don't Speak with Your Mouth Full

### B. Listen and number the pictures. p. 26

### C. Read and check True or False. p. 27

1. True      2. False      3. False

### Reading Time p. 29

1. Don't speak with your mouth full and cover your mouth when you cough.
2. [Example] Elbows off the table and sit up straight.

## Lesson 7 Places to Buy Things

### B. Read and match. p. 32

2. ©      3. ⓓ      4. ⓐ

## Lesson 8 Places to Find

### B. Listen and choose. p. 36

1. a    2. b    3. b    d. a

### C. Match, ask, and answer. p. 37

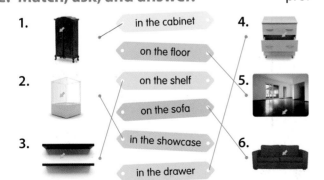

## Lesson 9 Kero Got a New Bat!

### B. Listen and number the pictures. p. 38

### C. Read and circle. p. 39

1. bats     2. sports shop     3. on the shelf

### Reading Time p. 41

1. It is to sell things you don't need.
2. [Example] I would sell my toys at flea markets.

## Lesson 10 Assessment Test 1

### Listening p. 42

**A.** 1. a   2. b   3. a   4. b   5. a   6. b

**B.** 1. c   2. b

### Speaking p. 43

**A.** 1. It is one hundred twenty dollars.
   2. No, they are on the shelf.
   3. Yes, I am. I would like some potato pizza.
   4. Sure.

**B.** ③ No, they are in the showcase.
   ② I'm looking for bats. Are they in the cabinet?

### Reading p. 44

**A.** 1. e   2. d   3. f   4. c   5. a   6. b

**B.** 1. True    2. False    3. True

### Writing p. 45

**A.** 1. music store   2. ninety   3. salt
   4. Chinese   5. in the drawer
   6. napkin   7. salad

**B.** 1. You can buy one at a sports shop.
   2. they are in the cabinet
   3. I want to go to an Italian restaurant.

## Lesson 11 At the Shop

**B. Read and choose.** p. 48

1. ⓓ    2. ⓑ    3. ⓒ    4. ⓐ

**C. Match, ask, and answer.** p. 49

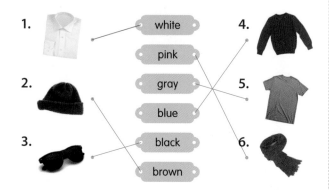

## Lesson 12 Starting Times

**B. Listen and write.** p. 52

1. 5, 10    2. 12, 00    3. 11, 40    4. 7, 15

**C. Ask, answer, and draw.** p. 53

## Lesson 13 My Baseball Game Begins at Twelve!

**B. Listen and number the pictures.** p. 54

**C. Read and circle.** p. 55

1. sports shop    2. blue    3. twelve

**Reading Time** p. 57

1. Earth Hour is a global event to save the Earth.
2. We turn off the lights for an hour from 8:30 p.m. to 9:30 p.m.

## Lesson 14 Asking for Reasons

**B. Listen and number.** p. 60

**a.** 2    **b.** 1    **c.** 4    **d.** 3

## Lesson 15 Making Suggestions

**B. Read and choose.** p. 64

1. ⓑ    2. ⓒ    3. ⓐ    4. ⓓ

**C. Go down the ladder. Then, ask and answer.** p. 65

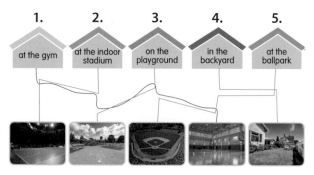

## Lesson 16 Playing Badminton on a Rainy Day

**B. Listen and number the pictures.** p. 66

**C. Read and answer the questions.** p. 67

1. a    2. b    3. b

**Reading Time** p. 69

1. The reason is that they work all day long to earn money.
2. [Example] We can save money and send it to the children.

# Lesson 17 Your Baseball Position
**B. Read and choose.**  p. 72

**C. Match, ask, and answer.**  p. 73

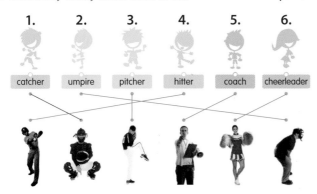

# Lesson 18 Does He Play Ice Hockey?
**B. Listen and check.**  p. 76

1. True   2. True   3. False   4. True

# Lesson 19 Kero Is a Pitcher!
**B. Listen and number the pictures.**  p. 78

**C. Read and check True or False.**  p. 79

1. True   2. False   3. True

**Reading Time**  p. 81

1. There are nine players on a team.

2. When the hitter misses the ball, the catcher catches it.

# Lesson 20 Assessment Test 2
Listening  p. 82

**A. 1.** b   **2.** a   **3.** b   **4.** a   **5.** a   **6.** b

**B. 1.** b   **2.** b

Speaking  p. 83

**A. 1.** Sounds great.
   **2.** Yes, he does.
   **3.** It begins at five ten.
   **4.** I have to water the flowers.

**B.** ② Sorry. I'm busy.
   ③ Why are you busy?
   ④ I have to cook dinner.

Reading  p. 84

**A. 1.** b   **2.** c   **3.** a   **4.** f   **5.** d   **6.** e

**B. 1.** True   **2.** True   **3.** False

Writing  p. 85

**A. 1.** pitcher   **2.** at the indoor stadium
   **3.** cook dinner   **4.** white
   **5.** go bowling   **6.** eleven forty
   **7.** hitter

**B. 1.** I like the brown one.
   **2.** It begins at twelve.
   **3.** I have to cook dinner.

# Workbook Answers

## Lesson 1 Choosing a Restaurant   pp. 4~5

**A.** 1. Let's eat out.
2. Which restaurant do you want to go to?
3. Sure, let's go.
4. I want to go to an Italian restaurant.

**B.** 1. Chinese   2. Indian   3. Japanese   4. Italian

**C.** 1. out   2. let's   3. Which   4. restaurant

**D.** 1. Which restaurant do, a Japanese restaurant
2. Which restaurant do, go to, to an Indian restaurant

## Lesson 2 At the Restaurant   pp. 6~7

**A.** 1. Are you ready to order?
2. I would like a salad.
3. Yes, I am.
4. Okay.

**B.** 1. potato pizza
2. spaghetti and meatballs
3. salad
4. garlic bread

**C.** 1. ready   2. am   3. like   4. some

**D.** 1. Are, to order, would, salad
2. Are, ready to order, would like, garlic bread

## Lesson 3 Kero Is at an Italian Restaurant   pp. 8~9

**A.** 1. Okay   2. Which, Italian
4. order   5. would

**B.** 1. I want to go to an Indian restaurant.
2. Are you ready to order?
3. Let's eat out.
4. I would like some potato pizza.

**Reading Time-Voca**
1. Italy   2. Mexico   3. the USA
4. India   5. France   6. Japan

## Lesson 4 Table Manners   pp. 10~11

**A.** 1. Don't speak with your mouth full.
2. Pass me the salt, please.
3. Cover your mouth when you cough.
4. Sure.

**B.** 1. napkin   2. salt   3. pepper   4. sugar

**C.** 1. full   2. Pass   3. Cover   4. napkin

**D.** 1. me the pepper
2. Pass me, napkin, please

## Lesson 5 Asking about Prices   pp. 12~13

**A.** 1. How was the food?   2. How much is it?
3. It was good.   4. It is ninety dollars.

**B.** 1. eighty   2. ninety   3. one hundred
4. one hundred twenty

**C.** 1. food   2. delicious   3. much   4. dollars

**D.** 1. How much, ninety dollars
2. How much is it, one hundred twenty dollars

## Lesson 6 Don't Speak with Your Mouth Full   pp. 14~15

**A.** 1. full   2. Pass   3. Cover
4. delicious   5. ninety

**B.** 1. How was the food?

2. Cover your mouth when you cough.

3. Pass me the sugar, please.

4. How much is it?

### Reading Time-Voca

1. blow     2. complain     3. full

4. cover     5. bite     6. sink

## Lesson 7 Places to Buy Things    pp. 16~17

**A.** 1. Oh, I have to buy a recorder.

2. Where can I buy a recorder?

3. Okay, let's go to buy one.

4. You can buy one at a sports shop.

**B.** 1. music store     2. stationery store

3. sports shop     4. department store

**C.** 1. recorder     2. buy

3. Where     4. music store

**D. Example.** Where

1. Where can I, at a sports shop

2. Where can I, buy one at a stationery store

## Lesson 8 Places to Find    pp. 18~19

**A.** 1. What can I do for you?

2. Are they in the cabinet?

3. I'm looking for bats.

4. No, they are on the shelf.

**B.** 1. on the shelf     2. in the showcase

3. in the drawer     4. in the cabinet

**C.** 1. What   2. looking   3. Are   4. showcase

**D.** 1. Are, in the drawer

2. Are they, they are in the cabinet

## Lesson 9 Kero Got a New Bat!    pp. 20~21

**A.** 1. bat    2. sports shop    3. looking for

4. cabinet, on the shelf

**B.** 1. Where can I buy a recorder?

2. No, they are in the showcase.

3. You can buy one at a stationery store.

4. Are they in the cabinet?

### Reading Time-Voca

1. flea market    2. magazine    3. furniture

4. garage sale    5. accessories    6. clothes

## Lesson 11 At the Shop    pp. 22~23

**A.** 1. There are so many recorders.

2. Which one do you like?

3. Yes, you're right.

4. I like the brown one.

**B.** 1. black     2. brown

3. blue     5. white

**C.** 1. There     2. right

3. Which     4. one

**D.** 1. Which one do, white one

2. Which one do you like, like the black one

## Lesson 12 Starting Times    pp. 24~25

**A.** 1. When is your baseball game?

2. When does it begin?

3. It's this Sunday.

4. It begins at seven fifteen.

**B.** 1. eleven forty     2. five ten

3. twelve     4. seven fifteen

**C.** 1. When     2. Sunday

3. begin     4. at

**D.** 1. When does, seven fifteen

2. When does it begin, begins at five ten

## Lesson 13 My Baseball Game Begins at Twelve! pp. 26~27

**A.** 1. many   2. blue
3. baseball   4. twelve
5. Sunday

**B.** 1. When does it begin?
2. I like the brown one.
3. When is your baseball game?
4. There are so many bats.

### Reading Time-Voca
1. light   2. hour
3. people   4. city
5. turn off   6. Earth

## Lesson 14 Asking for Reasons pp. 28~29

**A.** 1. Let's play the recorder together.
2. Why are you busy?
3. Sorry. I'm busy.
4. I have to go to the animal hospital.

**B.** 1. go to the animal hospital
2. water the flowers
3. do the laundry
4. cook dinner

**C.** 1. play   2. Sorry
3. busy   4. cook

**D.** 1. Why are, water the flowers
2. Why are you busy, have to do the laundry

## Lesson 15 Making Suggestions pp. 30~31

**A.** 1. It's raining, Henry.
2. Let's play baseball at the gym.
3. Oh, you're right.
4. Sounds good.

**B.** 1. on the playground
2. in the backyard
3. at the gym
4. at the indoor stadium

**C.** 1. raining   2. can't
3. at   4. great

**D.** 1. on the playground
2. play basketball in the backyard, Sounds

## Lesson 16 Playing Badminton on a Rainy Day pp. 32~33

**A.** 1. badminton   2. cook
3. raining   4. can't
5. great

**B.** 1. I have to go to the animal hospital.
2. It's raining!
3. Let's play badminton at the gym.
4. I'm busy.

### Reading Time-Voca
1. children   2. sick
3. poor   4. help
5. hungry   6. go to school

## Lesson 17 Your Baseball Position
pp. 34~35

**A.** 1. What's your position?
2. Are you a catcher, too?
3. I'm a pitcher.
4. No, I'm not. I'm a hitter.

**B.** 1. hitter   2. pitcher
3. umpire   4. catcher

**C.** **1.** position     **2.** catcher
    **3.** too     **4.** umpire

**D.** **1.** Are, an umpire
    **2.** Are you, too, a pitcher

## Lesson 18 Does He Play Ice Hockey?

pp. 36~37

**A.** **1.** Who is she?
    **2.** Does she play baseball?
    **3.** He's my friend Danny.
    **4.** No, he doesn't.

**B.** **1.** play ice hockey     **2.** play golf
    **3.** go bowling     **4.** play table tennis

**C.** **1.** Who     **2.** friend
    **3.** play     **4.** does

**D.** **1.** she go bowling, does
    **2.** he play table tennis, he does

## Lesson 19 Kero Is a Pitcher!
pp. 38~39

**A.** **1.** pitcher     **2.** catcher
    **3.** umpire     **4.** every day
    **5.** begins

**B.** **1.** Yes, he does.
    **2.** What's your position?
    **3.** He's my friend Timmy.
    **4.** I'm not, I'm a catcher.

### Reading Time-Voca
    **1.** baseball team     **2.** sign
    **3.** between     **4.** outfield
    **5.** catch     **6.** throw

# Final Test
# English Town Book 3

| 1. ④ | 2. ③ | 3. ⑤ | 4. ② | 5. ① |
|---|---|---|---|---|
| 6. ⑤ | 7. ② | 8. ③ | 9. ④ | 10. ① |
| 11. ② | 12. ③ | 13. ⑤ | 14. ② | 15. ① |
| 16. ④ | 17. ④ | 18. ④ | 19. Cover | |

**20.** playground, great

# Final Test

# English Town Book 3

| Class | Name | Score |
|---|---|---|
| | | /20 |

## Part 1- Listening

**[1-2] Look, listen, and choose the correct word.**

1
① ② ③ ④ ⑤

2
120
① ② ③ ④ ⑤

**[3-4] Listen and choose the correct picture.**

3
①
②
③

4
① ② ③
④ ⑤

**[5-6] Listen and choose the correct sentence.**

5
① ② ③ ④ ⑤

6
① ② ③ ④ ⑤

**[7-8] Listen and choose the correct picture.**

7
① ② ③
④ ⑤

8
① ② ③
④ ⑤

**[9-10] Look, listen, and choose the correct answer.**

9
① ② ③ ④ ⑤

10
① ② ③ ④ ⑤

## Part 2- Speaking

11 Listen and choose the wrong conversation.
① ② ③ ④ ⑤

12 Listen and choose the best response to the last sentence.
① ② ③ ④ ⑤

# Final Test_English Town Book 3

**[13-14] Choose the correct words for the blanks.**

**13**

> A: _____ in the cabinet?
> B: No, they are in the showcase.

① Do they    ② Where is    ③ Are you
④ Is it    ⑤ Are they

**14**

> A: _____
> B: I have to go to the animal hospital.

① When does it begin?
② Why are you busy?
③ What's your position?
④ Which one do you like?
⑤ Which restaurant do you want to go to?

**[15-16] Read and answer the questions.**

> A: When is your baseball game?
> B: It's this Saturday.
> A: _____ does it begin?
> B: It begins at eleven forty.

**15** What is the correct word for the blank?

① When    ② How    ③ Where
④ What    ⑤ Which

**16** When does the baseball game begin?

① 4:11    ② 11:14    ③ 11:50
④ 11:40    ⑤ 12:40

**[17-18] Read and answer the questions.**

> Sam: Hi, Kelly. _____ is he?
> Kelly: He is my brother Paul.
> Sam: He is very tall! Does he play basketball?
> Kelly: No, he doesn't. He plays ice hockey.

**17** What is the correct word for the blank?

① When    ② What    ③ Where
④ Who    ⑤ Which

**18** What is NOT true about the dialog?

① Paul is Kelly's brother.
② Paul plays ice hockey.
③ Paul is very tall.
④ Paul is a basketball player.
⑤ Sam and Kelly are talking about Paul.

**[19-20] Choose and write the correct words.**

> playground   well   speak   cover   great

**19** A: _____ your mouth when you
> cough.
> B: Okay.

**20** A: Let's play baseball on the _____.
> B: Sounds _____.

# ENGLISH TOWN

## FOR EVERYONE

### TOWN

**BOOK 3**

**WORKBOOK**

YBM

# ENGLiSH TOWN

FOR EVERYONE

BOOK

3

WORKBOOK

# Contents

# Choosing a Restaurant

## Let's Write

### A. Look, choose, and write.

① _____

Okay.

② _____

I want to go to an Italian restaurant.

Which restaurant do you want to go to?

Let's eat out.

③ _____

④ _____

- Sure, let's go.
- Let's eat out.
- Which restaurant do you want to go to?
- I want to go to an Italian restaurant.

## B. Write the words.

Italian  Chinese  Indian  Japanese

①  _____

②  _____

③  _____

④  _____

## C. Choose and write.

① Let's eat _____ .

② Sure, _____ go.

③ _____ restaurant do you want to go to?

④ I want to go to an Italian _____ .

let's
out
restaurant
which

## D. Look and write.

Example

A: _Which_ restaurant do you want to go to?

B: I want to go to an _Italian_ restaurant.

①

A: _____ _____ _____ you want to go to?

B: I want to go to _____ _____ _____ .

②

A: _____ _____ _____ you want to _____
_____ ?

B: I want to go _____ _____ _____ _____ .

# At the Restaurant

**Let's Write**

**A. Look, choose, and write.**

1. _____

Yes, I am.

2. _____

Okay.

3. _____

Are you ready to order?

I would like some spaghetti and meatballs.

4. _____

- Are you ready to order?
- Okay.
- I would like a salad.
- Yes, I am.

## B. Write the words.

1 _____

2 _____

3 _____

4 _____

## C. Choose and write.

1 Are you _____ to order?

2 Yes, I _____.

3 I would _____ a salad.

4 I would like _____ garlic bread.

am

some

ready

like

## D. Look and write.

Example

A: Are you ready to _order_?

B: Yes, I am. I would like some _potato_ _pizza_.

A: Okay.

1

A: _____ you ready _____ _____?

B: Yes, I am. I _____ like a _____.

A: Okay.

2

A: _____ you _____ _____ _____?

B: Yes, I am. I _____ _____ some _____
_____.

A: Okay.

# Kero Is at an Italian Restaurant

**Let's Write**

## A. Write the words and number the pictures.

**1**  Mom: Let's eat out.

Kero and Kiki: _____.

**2**  Mom: _____ restaurant do you want to go to?

Kiki: I want to go to an _____ restaurant.

Kero: I want to go to a Chinese restaurant.

**3**  Kero and Kiki: No way!

**4**  Waiter: Are you ready to _____?

Mom: Yes, I am. I would like a salad.

**5**  Kiki: I _____ like some spaghetti and meatballs.

Kero: I would like some potato pizza.

Waiter: Okay.

order

would

Italian

which

okay

## B. Unscramble and complete the dialogs.

**1** A: Which restaurant do you want to go to?

B: _____

( an / Indian / to / I / go / to / restaurant / want / . )

**2** A: _____

( order / to / you / ready / are / ? )

B: Yes, I am.

**3** A: _____

( eat / out / let's / . )

B: Okay.

**4** A: _____

( some / I / potato pizza / like / would / . )

B: Okay.

## Reading Time – Voca

● **Write the words.**

1.  Napoli Pizza from

_____

2.  Tacos from

_____

3.  Doughnuts from

_____

4.  Curry from

_____

5.  Croissant from

_____

6.  Sushi from

_____

Italy

India

France

Mexico

the USA

Japan

# Table Manners

**Let's Write**

## A. Look, choose, and write.

**①** _____

Okay.

**②** _____

Sure.

Pass me a napkin, please.

**④** _____

Okay.

**③** _____

_____

- Don't speak with your mouth full.
- Cover your mouth when you cough.
- Sure.
- Pass me the salt, please.

**B.** **Write the words.**

①

②

③

④

_____   _____   _____   _____

**C.** **Choose and write.**

① Don't speak with your mouth _____.

② _____ me the salt, please.

③ _____ your mouth when you cough.

④ Pass me a _____, please.

napkin
pass
full
cover

**D.** **Look and write.**

Example

A: Pass me the _salt_, please.

B: Sure.

①

A: Pass _____ _____ _____, please.

B: Sure.

②

A: _____ _____ a _____, _____.

B: Sure.

## Lesson 5 Asking about Prices

**Let's Write**

**A. Look, choose, and write.**

① _____

It was delicious.

It is eighty dollars.

② _____

How was the food?

③ _____

How much is it?

BIG SALE 50% OFF

90 dollars

④ _____

- How much is it?
- It was good.
- How was the food?
- It is ninety dollars.

**B. Write the words.**

ninety   one hundred   eighty
one hundred twenty

①  $80

_____

②  $90

_____

③  $100

_____

④  $120

_____

**C. Choose and write.**

① How was the _____?

② It was _____.

③ How _____ is it?

④ It is eighty _____.

dollars
delicious
food
much

**D. Look and write.**

Example
80

A: How much is it?

B: It is _eighty_ dollars.

①
90

A: _____ _____ is it?

B: It is _____ _____.

② 120

A: _____ _____ _____ _____?

B: It is _____ _____ _____ _____.

# Don't Speak with Your Mouth Full

**Let's Write**

## A. Write the words and number the pictures.

**1** Mom: Don't speak with your mouth _____.

Kero: Okay.

**2** Kiki: _____ me the pepper, please.

Dad: Sure.

**3** Mom: _____ your mouth when you cough.

**4** Dad: How was the food?

Kiki: It was _____.

**5** Mom: How much is it?

Waiter: It is _____ dollars.

| |
|---|
| ninety |
| delicious |
| full |
| pass |
| cover |

## B. Unscramble and complete the dialogs.

**1** A: _____

( food / was / how / the / ? )

B: It was delicious.

**2** A: _____

( cough / your / cover / you / mouth / when / . )

B: Okay.

**3** A: _____

( the / me / please / pass / sugar / . / , )

B: Sure.

**4** A: _____

( much / is / how / it / ? )

B: It is one hundred dollars.

## Reading Time – Voca

- **Write the words.**

1.  _____

2.  _____

3.  _____

4.  _____

5.  _____

6.  _____

sink

full

complain

blow

bite

cover

# Places to Buy Things

**Let's Write**

## A. Look, choose, and write.

① _____

Okay, let's go to buy one.

② _____

You can buy one at a music store.

Oh, I have to buy a bat.

Where can I buy a bat?

Sports shop

③ _____

④ _____

- Oh, I have to buy a recorder.
- Where can I buy a recorder?
- Okay, let's go to buy one.
- You can buy one at a sports shop.

## B. Write the words.

music store    sports shop
department store    stationery store

①  _____

②  _____

③  _____

④  _____

## C. Choose and write.

where
recorder
music store
buy

① Oh, I have to buy a _____ .

② Okay, let's go to _____ one.

③ _____ can I buy a recorder?

④ You can buy one at a _____ .

## D. Look and write.

Example
department store

A: _____ can I buy a scarf?

B: You can buy one at a <u>department</u> <u>store</u> .

① sports shop

A: _____ _____ _____ buy a ball?

B: You can buy one _____ _____ _____

_____ .

② stationery store

A: _____ _____ _____ buy a stapler?

B: You can _____ _____ _____

_____ _____ .

# Places to Find

**Let's Write**

## A. Look, choose, and write.

① _____

I'm looking for recorders.

② _____

No, they are in the showcase.

What can I do for you?

Are they in the box?

③ _____

④ _____

- No, they are on the shelf.
- I'm looking for bats.
- Are they in the cabinet?
- What can I do for you?

## B. Write the words.

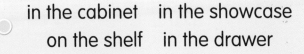
in the cabinet    in the showcase
on the shelf    in the drawer

**1**

_____

**2**

_____

**3**

_____

**4**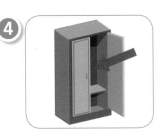

_____

## C. Choose and write.

**1** _____ can I do for you?

**2** I'm _____ for recorders.

**3** _____ they in the cabinet?

**4** No, they are in the _____ .

looking
are
what
showcase

## D. Look and write.

Example

A: Are they in the cabinet?

B: No, they are in the  _showcase_ .

**1**

A: _____ they in the showcase?

B: No, they are _____ _____ _____ .

**2**

A: _____ _____ on the shelf?

B: No, _____ _____ _____ _____

_____ .

# Kero Got a New Bat!

**Let's Write**

## A. Write the words and number the pictures.

**①** Kero: I have to buy a _____.

Dad: Okay, let's go to buy one.

**②** Kero: Where can I buy a bat?

Dad: You can buy one at a _____.

**③** Clerk: What can I do for you?

Kero: I'm _____ bats.

**④** Kero: Are they in the _____?

Clerk: No, they are _____.

sports shop

bat

cabinet

looking for

on the shelf

## B. Unscramble and complete the dialogs.

**1** A: _____

( recorder / can / where / buy / I / a / ? )

B: You can buy one at a music store.

**2** A: Are they on the shelf?

B: _____

( showcase / in / they / no / are / the / . / , )

**3** A: Where can I buy a stapler?

B: _____

( at / can / stationery store / buy / one / a / you / . )

**4** A: I'm looking for bats. _____

( the / they / cabinet / are / in / ? )

B: No, they are in the box.

### Reading Time – Voca

- **Write the words.**

1.
_____

2.
_____

3.
_____

4.
_____

5.
_____

6.
_____

magazine

furniture

accessories

clothes

garage sale

flea market

## At the Shop

### Let's Write

**A. Look, choose, and write.**

① _____

Yes, you're right.

② _____

I like the white one.

There are so many bats.

Which one do you like?

③ _____

④ _____

- Which one do you like?
- I like the brown one.
- There are so many recorders.
- Yes, you're right.

**B. Write the words.**

○ white   brown   black   blue ○

**①**

**②**

**③**

**④**

_____   _____   _____   _____

**C. Choose and write.**

**①** _____ are so many recorders.

**②** Yes, you're _____ .

**③** _____ one do you like?

**④** I like the white _____ .

○ ○
there
one
which
right
○ ○

**D. Look and write.**

Example

A: _Which_ one do you like?

B: I like the _blue_ one.

**①**

A: _____ _____ _____ you like?

B: I like the _____ _____ .

**②**

A: _____ _____ _____ _____ ?

B: I _____ _____ _____ _____ .

# Starting Times

**Let's Write**

**A.** Look, choose, and write.

1. _____
   It's this Sunday.

2. _____
   It begins at twelve.

3. _____
   When is your concert?

4. _____
   When does it begin?

---

• It's this Sunday.
• When is your baseball game?
• It begins at seven fifteen.
• When does it begin?

## B. Write the words.

**1**

**2**

**3**

**4**

_____   _____   _____   _____

## C. Choose and write.

**1** _____ is your baseball game?

**2** It's this _____ .

**3** When does it _____ ?

**4** It begins _____ twelve.

at
begin
Sunday
when

## D. Look and write.

Example

12:00.

A:  _When_ does it begin?

B:  It begins at _twelve_ .

**1** 7:15.

A:  _____ _____ it begin?

B:  It begins at _____ _____ .

**2** 5:10.

A:  _____ _____ _____ _____ ?

B:  It _____ _____ _____ _____ .

# My Baseball Game Begins at Twelve!

**Let's Write**

**A.** **Write the words and number the pictures.**

**1** Kero: There are so _____ bats.

Clerk: Yes, you're right.

**2** Clerk: Which one do you like?

Kero: I like the _____ one.

I will use it in my baseball game.

**3** Clerk: When is your _____ game?

Kero: It is this Sunday.

**4** Mom: When does it begin?

Kero: It begins at _____.

**5** Kiki: Mom, I have a concert this _____.

It begins at three.

Mom: I know. I know. I'll be there.

Sunday

baseball

many

twelve

blue

## B. Unscramble and complete the dialogs.

**1** A: _____

( it / when / begin / does / ? )

B: It begins at twelve.

**2** A: Which one do you like?

B: _____

( brown / the / like / one / I / . )

**3** A: _____

( game / is / baseball / when / your / ? )

B: It is this Sunday.

**4** A: _____

( many / are / so / there / bats / . )

B: Yes, you're right.

### Reading Time – Voca

- **Write the words.**

1.  _____

2.  _____

3.  _____

4.  _____

5.  _____

6.  _____

people

turn off

Earth

light

city

hour

# Asking for Reasons

**Let's Write**

## A. Look, choose, and write.

① _____

Sorry. I'm busy.

② _____

I have to cook dinner.

Let's play baseball together.

③ _____

Why are you busy?

④ _____
   _____

- Why are you busy?
- Sorry. I'm busy.
- Let's play the recorder together.
- I have to go to the animal hospital.

**B. Write the words.**

cook dinner    go to the animal hospital
do the laundry    water the flowers

**①**
_____

**②**
_____

**③**
_____

**④**
_____

**C. Choose and write.**

**①** Let's _____ the recorder together.

**②** _____. I'm busy.

**③** Why are you _____?

**④** I have to _____ dinner.

cook
play
sorry
busy

**D. Look and write.**

Example

A: _Why_ are you busy?

B: I have to _cook_ _dinner_.

**①**

A: _____ _____ you busy?

B: I have to _____ _____ _____.

**②**

A: _____ _____ _____ _____?

B: I _____ _____ _____ _____ _____.

# Making Suggestions

**Let's Write**

## A. Look, choose, and write.

- It's raining, Henry.
- Oh, you're right.
- Sounds good.
- Let's play baseball at the gym.

## B. Write the words.

at the gym    at the indoor stadium
on the playground    in the backyard

**1**

_____

**2**

_____

**3**

_____

**4**

_____

## C. Choose and write.

**1** It's _____, Henry.

**2** Oh, no. We _____ play baseball.

**3** Let's play baseball _____ the gym.

**4** Sounds _____.

can't
great
at
raining

## D. Look and write.

Example

A: Let's play basketball <u>at  the  gym</u>.

B: Sounds great.

**1**

A: Let's play basketball _____ _____ _____.

B: Sounds great.

**2**

A: Let's _____ _____ _____ _____

_____.

B: _____ great.

# Playing Badminton on a Rainy Day

**Let's Write**

**A.** **Write the words and number the pictures.**

① Kero: Let's play _____, Mom.

Mom: Sorry. I'm busy.

② Kero: Why are you busy?

Mom: I have to _____ dinner.

③ Kero: Let's play badminton, Dad.

Dad: Sounds great!

Kiki: Look! It's _____!

④ Kero: Oh, no! We _____ play badminton.

Dad: Why not?

⑤ Dad: Let's play badminton at the gym.

Kero: Sounds _____. Let's go!

badminton

great

cook

can't

raining

... cook dinner.

## B. Unscramble and complete the dialogs.

**1** A: Why are you busy?

B: _____

( have / to / hospital / go / the / I / animal / to / . )

**2** A: Look! _____

( raining / it's / ! )

B: Oh, no! We can't play baseball.

**3** A: _____

( the / play / gym / at / let's / badminton / . )

B: Sounds great.

**4** A: Let's play badminton together.

B: Sorry. _____

( busy / I'm / . )

### Reading Time – Voca

- **Write the words.**

1.  _____

2.  _____

3.  _____

4.  _____

5.  _____

6.  _____

| hungry |
| --- |
| help |
| poor |
| children |
| sick |
| go to school |

Lesson 16   **33**

# Your Baseball Position

## Let's Write

### A. Look, choose, and write.

① _____

I'm a catcher.

② _____

No, I'm not. I'm an umpire.

③ _____

Are you a pitcher, too?

What's your position?

④ _____

- Are you a catcher, too?
- I'm a pitcher.
- What's your position?
- No, I'm not. I'm a hitter.

**B. Write the words.**

catcher   umpire   pitcher   hitter

 **2**

**3**

**4**

_____   _____   _____   _____

**C. Choose and write.**

**1** What's your _____?

**2** I'm a _____.

**3** Are you a catcher, _____?

**4** No, I'm not. I'm an _____.

too
position
catcher
umpire

**D. Look and write.**

Example

A: Are you a hitter, too?

B: No, I'm not. I'm <u>a  catcher</u>.

**1**

A: _____ you a hitter, too?

B: No, I'm not. I'm _____ _____.

**2**

A: _____ _____ a hitter, _____?

B: No, I'm not. I'm _____ _____.

# Does He Play Ice Hockey?

## Let's Write

### A. Look, choose, and write.

- No, he doesn't.
- He's my friend Danny.
- Does she play baseball?
- Who is she?

## B. Write the words.

play ice hockey    play table tennis
play golf    go bowling

 ① _____

 ② _____

 ③ _____

 ④ _____

## C. Choose and write.

① _____ is she?

② She's my _____ Kelly.

③ Does she _____ baseball?

④ Yes, she _____.

play
does
friend
who

## D. Look and write.

Example

A: Does he _play_ _ice_ _hockey_?
B: Yes, he does.

 ①

A: Does _____ _____ _____?
B: Yes, she _____.

 ②

A: Does _____ _____ _____ _____?
B: Yes, _____ _____.

# Kero Is a Pitcher!

**Let's Write**

**A.** **Write the words and number the pictures.**

**①** Kiki: What's your position?

Kero: I'm a _____.

**②** Kiki: Are you a pitcher, too?

Friend: No, I'm not. I'm a _____.

**③** Dad: Who is he?

Kero: He's my teacher Mr. Smith. He is an _____.

**④** Kiki: Does he play baseball _____?

Kero: Yes, he does.

**⑤** Kero: It _____! I have to go!

Dad, Mom and Kiki: Good luck!

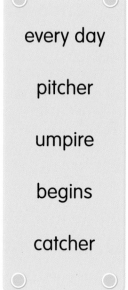

every day

pitcher

umpire

begins

catcher

# B. Unscramble and complete the dialogs.

**1** A: Does he play baseball?

B: _____
( does / he / yes / . / , )

**2** A: _____
( position / what's / your / ? )

B: I'm a catcher.

**3** A: Who is he?

B: _____
( friend / my / Timmy / he's / . )

**4** A: Are you a pitcher, too?

B: No, _____. _____
( not / I'm )                    ( a / I'm / catcher / . )

## Reading Time – Voca

- **Write the words.**

1.  _____

2.  _____

3.  _____

4.  _____

5.  _____

6. _____

throw

catch

sign

baseball
team

outfield

between

Memo

# ENGLiSH TOWN

**BOOK 3**

## ENGLiSH TOWN BOOK 3

*English Town* is a spoken English course comprised of a series of 9 books, specifically designed for elementary school students.

- Learning English in a communicative way and in an easy manner
- Focused approach to new words, expressions, and dialogs
- Fun to sing and chant together
- Simple but effective games and activities
- Exciting stories

### Components

· Student Book

· Workbook

· Final Test

· Teacher's Guide including teaching resources

· Online (www.ybmenglishtown.com)

  Interactive e-book for teachers and students

  E-learning for self-study

 www.ybmenglishtown.com

YBM